D1490813

37653015006656
Main   NonFiction
811.54 BOISSEAU
A Sunday in God-years :
poems

APR   2009

CENTRAL ARKANSAS LIBRARY SYSTEM
LITTLE ROCK PUBLIC LIBRARY
100 ROCK STREET
LITTLE ROCK, ARKANSAS

GAYLORD

ALSO BY MICHELLE BOISSEAU

No Private Life
Understory
Trembling Air

A Sunday
in God-Years

POEMS BY
MICHELLE BOISSEAU

The University of Arkansas Press
Fayetteville
2009

Copyright © 2009 by Michelle Boisseau

All rights reserved
Manufactured in the United States of America

ISBN-10: 1-55728-901-8
ISBN-13: 978-1-55728-901-8

13 12 11 10 09   5 4 3 2 1

Designed by Liz Lester

⊛ The paper used in this publication meets the minimum requirements of
the American National Standard for Permanence of Paper for Printed
Library Materials Z39.48-1984.

LIBRARY OF CONGRESS CATALOGING-IN-PUBLICATION DATA

Boisseau, Michelle, 1955–
      A Sunday in God-years : poems / by Michelle Boisseau.
         p.   cm.
      ISBN-13: 978-1-55728-901-8 (pbk. : alk. paper)
      ISBN-10: 1-55728-901-8 (pbk. : alk. paper)
      I. Title.
      PS3552.O555S86   2009
      811'.54—dc22
                            2008046458

for Pat

CENTRAL ARKANSAS LIBRARY SYSTEM
LITTLE ROCK PUBLIC LIBRARY
100 ROCK STREET
LITTLE ROCK, ARKANSAS 72201

[D]uring the Tertiary ages . . . a warm and genial climate prevailed from the Gulf to the Arctic Sea; the Canadian highlands were higher, but the Rocky Mountains lower and less broad. Most of the continent exhibited an undulating surface, rounded hills and broad valleys covered with forests grander than any of the present day, or wide expanses of rich savannah, over which roamed countless herds of animals, many of gigantic size, of which our present meager fauna retains but a few dwarfed representatives. Noble rivers flowed through plains and valleys, and sea-like lakes, broader and more numerous than those the continent now bears, diversified the scenery. Through unnumbered ages the seasons ran their ceaseless course, the sun rose and set, moons waxed and waned over this fair land, but no human eye was there to mark its beauty, nor human intellect to control and use its exuberant fertility. Flowers opened their many colored petals on meadow and hill-side, and filled the air with their perfumes, but only for the delectation of the wandering bee. Fruits ripened in the sun, but there was no hand there to pluck, nor any speaking tongue to taste. Birds sang in the trees, but for no ears but their own. The surface of lake or river whitened by no sail, nor furrowed by any prow but the breast of the water-foul; and the far-reaching shores echoed no sound but the dash of the waves and the lowing of the herds that slacked their thirst in the crystal waters.

—J. S. NEWBERRY

Location's narrow way is for Ourselves—
Unto the Dead
There's no Geography—

—DICKINSON, F476, J489

Grateful acknowledgment is made to the editors of the following journals in whose pages some of these poems first appeared, sometimes in earlier versions: *Cincinnati Review* ("Larger than Life"), *Crab Orchard Review* ("Outskirts of Lynchburg"), *Fourth River* ("Flying with the Eyes of a Satellite"), *Gettysburg Review* ("Not to Mention All This Ferrous Fructiferousness," "When I Consider"), *Green Mountains Review* ("South Dakota Field Trip"), *Kenyon Review* ("Die Zwei Ist Zweifel"), *National Poetry Review* ("Pertinacious Seedheads"), *New Letters* ("Across the Borderlands, the Wind"), *Ploughshares* ("A Sunday in God-Years," "Monstrance," "Eighteenth-Century Boisseau Farmhouse"), *Poetry* ("The Good," "Time Done Is Dark"), *Shenandoah: The Washington and Lee University Review* ("After a While Time Passed"), *Sou'wester* ("Ode to the Tongue"), *TriQuarterly*, a publication of Northwestern University ("Inkling"), *upstreet* ("Recriminating Rags of Sunlight"), *Women's Review of Books* ("Birthday," "A Genius for Silence").

I owe a debt of thanks to Andrew Boisseau whose research and documentation on the Boisseaus helped clarify and direct the development of this book. Thanks also to the Library of Virginia, the Virginia Historical Society, the Ohio Historical Society, and the Library of Congress, whose holdings prompted some of these poems. "Found Poem" is on the Ohio Historical Society's website "The African-American Experience in Ohio"; many of the nineteenth-century maps cited are in both Virginian and Congressional collections. "Outskirts of Lynchburg," an early version of this poem was part of a commission by the Kemper Museum of Contemporary Art as a response to Jennifer Steinkamp's "Eye Catching" and other installations. A grant from the University of Missouri Research Board supported a leave to focus on this book. Thanks to the Department of English at the University of Missouri-Kansas City for travel funds. Thanks to Tina Niemi and Ray Coveney for help with geology questions. Many generous readers have given me encouragement, including Randall Mann, Robert Stewart, Jeff Greene, Paul Nelson, Christopher Buckley, Robin Becker, and, my husband, Tom Stroik, whose crankiness as a poetry reader I rely on. And special thanks to Al Young, who years ago looked at an early version of "A Reckoning," pointed at the runaway slave notice and told me to start over with it.

Cover image: Digital Collage by Kati Toivanen, 2008. The layers of this collage include details from G. F. Gilmer, "Map of Amelia Co., Virginia," 1864; runaway slave notice, the *Richmond Enquirer,* 1834; death notice and obituary, Fannie P. Boisseau, 1906, pasted inside a damaged book; muster roll, Virginia Cavalry, Co. G., Reg. 1, 1864; will of Priscilla Boisseau, 1856; notice of court case, *American Constitution* (newspaper), 1835; image of sun, NASA, 2006.

CONTENTS

II.

III.

A Sunday in God-Years

Birthday

A current strokes the pear tree and a fall
 of petals feathers the asphalt

and confettis my hair. The afternoon
 is full of exuberant ruin,

of beauty dissolved in the pushing forth
 of small hard fruit. In the old story

a sparrow crosses the mead hall, then flies
 out the other window: that's life,

a frantic flight across a crackling room
 where the clan feasts, harps gleam and the storm

is carefully forgotten. From dark freeze
 to freezing dark. But in between

this gorgeous kingdom. The transitory.

I.

A Sunday in God-Years

Like someone trying to nap in a room
with a glaring terrarium
God rolls over,
but before he resumes his dream
where he's a lover
decked out in a sunbeam
he glances at the blue planet
he made, at continents crashing
and mountains popping up, at sheets of dirt
settling in streams and streams
settling in oceans that slide back
like bedcovers and after stacks
of pressing epochs give birth

in an outcrop to this ragged chunk
of limestone I plucked
from a wall fading into the woods
of Northern Kentucky,
Ordovician, half a billion years old.
It was the common rock of my childhood,
what we pried from yards and pulled
from creeks to flush out crawdads
scuttling beneath. That's an hour's drive
and forty years ago, on the north side

of the Ohio. River Jordan. Promised Land.
Fine heft, a good fit to my hand,
the rock's finger notches are the curves
of river bends on a map—it's shaped
like Kentucky—and here's the turn
the river takes, *wade*
in the water, on its way

north from Maysville, here a cove
where a runaway could hide—
her child slung in a shawl—studying the floes
until the moon set and she could plunge
across the bobbing ice
to board, *sweet chariot,* the train of trudging—
corn fields, torches, disquieting towns, huddling
in root cellars by day, then in the hull
of a midnight boat slipping across Lake
Erie. The rock I slid from the wall
was stacked here by a slave. And slaves
felled trees, broke sod, and cut the stone
for foundations they couldn't own.

Up on the ancient hill the grand old house
they built is solitary now.

The clutter of shacks for those who worked
snow and swelter, blaze and night
have long been erased as eyesores
although the played out double-wides
along the road tell a revised story.
And as for me, a middle-aged white
woman, I didn't have to care
who'd notice me helping myself
to these grainy eons, plunder
imbedded with the trails and shells
of creatures seen by no eye although carelessly
glanced long ago through warm shallow
seas by a younger sun.

A Reckoning

1. The Debt

To the two strong trees, the well-screwed hooks, the
ropes, what does the hammock owe?

The portico, to the cut stone?

The groaning board, the roast, the butter, and gloaming
jams appear to speak in a register beyond dog
whistles. Who can hear forests and cattle, briars
and caramelized steam?

What does the storm sculling across the continent owe
the ocean?

Second-growth? At least third, maybe fourth. In the
woods the developer's crew stands around a hole.
The idling machines say hurry, hurry. Someone
clinks a shovel at something in the backhoe's
bucket. Tibia. Someone sizes up how many and
much. Glances are exchanged, tamping down,
tamping down, and the machines start up again.

In the courthouse, books as big as tables speak in lacy
script. What do you owe when you find your
name on a parchment deed?

2. Ruminator

Don't misunderstand.
I am the cow. This is my field,
my golden meadow. This my murky pond
where I ruminate and switch flies.

I eat the grass. The dry seeds skitter,
meander on the breeze and drop
from birds. Birds pick at bronze
droppings in the grass I eat.

Don't continue
to misunderstand there is a cow,
there is a field.

I am the field, the wavering meadow
I eat, the murky pond
I shamble to and drink,
flanks steaming.

　　　* * *

No one can remember
the forests, forests without
understory, looming tip to tip.

The green shade.

No one remembers the trees
dragged away
became lumber and great fleets
went under.

In the morning the flat ocean
glowing under the sun
and nothing new.

*   *   *

No one remembers the ship
limped into Charleston, a fired cannon
announced the arrival and a pilot boat
started out, but the harbor was already
awake to the shipment. Before dawn
they could smell it coming.

La Rochelle. Calabar. St. Kitts.
Providence. Liverpool. Richmond.

Clover to clover bloom, port to port,
bees gathering honey, the great fleets
sailed round and great cities rose.

The estates are still famous.
The good graces, ringing forges, teas
under lock and key, nimble servants.

    * * *

Cows dot the lawns. Around a bend
chimneys sprout from a mountain
of roofs. Windows slowly amber
in the evening sun. Behind
a line of trees, the cabins
lengthen in the shadow tide.

Are you arriving in the carriage?
Or around back in a wagon?

Imported, like the cow or honey bee,
sweet potato or daffodil, soon you belong
where you find yourself. Children,
grandchildren. Broken staves nailed
over a chink. Sugar in the silver service. Gold

leaves curing in the barns.
And the cow lumbers into the pond,
tears sour grass and murks the water.

3. No Trespassing. Violators Will Be
   Prosecuted, etc.

A road of industrial gravel staggers
under the locked gate I climb, under
the second gate I swing beneath.

Drizzle sticks like cotton lint to junk trees and scrub.

And around the bend, a clearing, opening onto . . .
Nope, not The House Where They Lived!

No be-lilaced cellar hole buzzing
like a hornet's nest with ancient meaning.
Nothing to weep over. No granite knees—
even the rocks aren't local, trucked in, dumped.

Instead, big as an airplane hangar,
a garage for backhoes and spreaders turns up
where the big house might have stood.

How many cabins would they have required
for the three score people they held
as slaves? This time next year
the trees will have been knocked aside
like incidents and the driveways poured.

I cowl my camera as the rain picks up
and video the view they didn't have—
across the Appomattox smoke sputters from
a single-wide trailer—thumbtack stuck in a tree.

4. Meanwhile

The year Whistler was born and Coleridge died;
the year Lincoln rode into Springfield
a fresh assemblyman, and hansom cabs
of bachelors began speeding around London;
the year Pushkin's *Queen of Spades*
appeared, an ink-smeared boy Whitman
set type against agitators, McCormick
patented his reaper, and mobs combed
Philadelphia burning out blacks
and abolitionists; the year what's now
Oklahoma, Kansas, and Nebraska
became Indian Territory and ragged
bands of Shawnee were run out of Ohio;
the year Emerson struck the gold vein
of his style and fell in love with Lydia;
the year on the quiet, with old spelling books,
Frederick Douglass conducted school
for fellow slaves was the year my mother's
great-grandfather, a boy in Pennsylvania
studied his Bible by daylight and lamplight
and my father's great-grandfather wrote out
a notice and trotted the dusty roads
of Virginia to place it in the paper:

5. Reward

$20 REWARD.—Ran away from the subscriber, on the night of the 29th of June, a negro man named, GIBSON, about 23 or 24 years of age, five feet eight or nine inches high, rather spare, of a dark complexion, very polite when spoken to. He carried off all his clothing, consisting of three pair of cotton, one pair of dark yarn, and a pair of green corduroy pantaloons, one blue cloth coat, and two hats; one a good wool hat, and the other a fur hat, with crape around it. I suspect he is either in Richmond, where he has been heretofore hired in a Tobacco Factory, or in the neighborhood of Mr. Richard Gregory's, near the Half-way House, where his father lives. I will give twenty dollars for the said Negro man if delivered to me near Chesterfield Court House, or committed to Jail, so that I can obtain him again.

July 4.   **PETER F. BOISSEAU.**

—The *Richmond Enquirer*, July 11, 1834

6. The Subscriber

The dipper dropped by the well, a footprint
among the climbing beans, the uncertain figure
inked in the mirror before the lamp is lit,
everywhere I look I read his signature.
A fellow loping along the road, his shadow
bouncing beside him. Or when I waited
for the ferry, across the river his sad
eyes and watchful smile printed on another boy's face.
He befriends the shadows of trees. His gait,
that slouch hat and his way of crushing
the brim when something strikes him strange.
I even started at a white man at supper
in a tavern. The thorough way the man
licked his spoon called up my Gibson's manner.
Though every Negro here to the Half-way
House says they can't say they've seen him and can't
recollect last time they did, I know
he's out there, bedded down in the woods, maybe
sidling into the barn when it storms, owing
his meals to raided orchards and stealing
toward our windows to haunt us as we sleep.

Expecting no luck like every other time,
I'm rounding the corner to the factory

and nearly leap out of my boots. It's him,
stretched bold as you please across some sacks
and I'm on him and he's hollering, *Mercy,*
Mercy as my cane snaps across his back,
my foot greets his head. When I go to turn
him over, his arm feels too beefy, too slack
the skin around his neck. Blood is darkening
the stream of piping along his collar. Something like
Gibson's coat. Two boys loading lumber in a cart
catch me looking around and style
themselves reading the grain in a board.
Sleeping in the day. This one was a laggard.

7. Catalogue

On the old map, roads end at the county line,
rivers snap like branches in an ice storm.
A gray blank islands the county
the way a halo of disappearance conceals

the man who fled a Boisseau farm.
Escaped? Captured? Sold south?
Undocumented. Rivers of unknowns
wash out his trail, leaving me the dry

marshes of archives. Holes and time-traps.
I wander this heated, clacking terrain
(microfilm flapping on the take-up reel)
collecting paper triumphs:

the soundings taken from land patents
(640 acres in 1756),
the reckonings of census and slave lists
(1500 acres in 1840, 56 slaves),

the sick victories from deciphering
the loops and strokes of handwritten wills:

8. Two Wills in Old Virginia

Of Sarah W. Baugh Boisseau, 1820: "I give and bequeath unto my daughter Priscilla G. Boisseau for and during the term of her natural life the following slaves, to wit, Matt, Tom, Busheba, and Little Suey and her infant child Iris, also the large bed, bedstead and bureau in my chamber."

Of Priscilla Hill Boisseau, 1856. "I give and bequeath to my grand-daughter Elizabeth R. Gibbs, my Negro girl Emily and her child Elie together with the future increase of the said slave Emily to his and her heirs forever."

9. Apologies

only *only account for that which they do not alter.*

                                        —BENJAMIN DISRAELI

The traffic of a sentimental novel
guides the runaway Gibson
past drunk patrols, through snake-rippling
swamps riddled with the ironic slow

butterfly. Days of running till below the Falls
he spots a British vessel in the fog,
on deck a disciple of Wilberforce
avid to smuggle him cinematically

across an ocean brimming with moon-roads,
inalienable rights and speaking tours.
Freedom is hard-won, but done. Sizzling platters
are carried in. Grab a chair and sit down.

Good gracious! Look at all this food.
Everyone finds a place at the table. Captain
and cook, shipper and shipped. Gibson's
great-great-grandchildren. And Little Suey's.

And me, grandchild who makes herself the hero
since she's the teller of this tale. I writhe
and what of it? How can I begin to recount
the sins, a million ships on every ocean?

10. Spear-Side and Distaff

The new curls from the old and the old rots
underfoot. Whoever came up with *tree?*
when family's a swamp, messy woods
good for getting lost, for stillness lost
in the clack of branches. What's that? Nothing.
And nothing again. Echoes, the soundings
of falling things, skirmishes of the unseen.

No one but me has come this way lately,
touched the runnels of bark, smelled the sweetness
of decay and slapped impediments
glinting like spider silk along the trail.
From him the slope of my nose, from her
freckles. And who's responsible for these
lead moods? Boisseau, Parham, Hill,

Bradley, Fitzpatrick, Holt, Holmes,
and I'm square in seventeenth-century
Virginia where the hush grows huge and sulky
as a scolded jury. And the evidence?
Impurely circumstantial. The circumstances?
Dangling husks that blur the branches, the way
the fallen cushion and obliterate.

11. Brown Study

Here three shades of white exchange thoughts.
The trampled snow talks to the icy river
and the low sky answers back. As it thaws,
the border muddies underfoot. Rocks shift

their attention and give way though each night's
general freeze shuts them down, a border town
under siege. Sky and ice, water and ice,
land and ice. It's fine to think we were formed

from mud. It's fine pictures of rivers favor
them bounding toward us (because the retreating
river is too sad, it runs away, waves
turn their backs on us). That the sky is fleet

is helpful. The earth turns. Rivers run like people,
far and fast as they can to taste the sea.

12. Field Guide to North American Guilt

Outcroppings of the oldest forms
have weathered into mountain stubs,
blunt incisors of a blind dog
the household skirts around. The worn

hill spills its gravel which is chewed
and smoothed in riverbeds and sported
along, burrs on the fur of currents,
and with silt, shells, bugs, tracks, and spume

laid in oceans. Impressed with time. Scarred.
Or driven deep under to boil.
And sometimes, rarely, it is tamed,
expressed like rubies from feldspar,

the clear, crimson crystal of shame.

13. Before the Age of Aerial Bombardment
Shenandoah Valley, October, 1864

Detail, abstraction, creation.
In the flying dream I glide above the scorch
and guns, brooding over the fields
as I form the world from an old battle map.

Burnt Mill   *J. Howell*   School-House
Widow Stickley   ROSSER 11. P.M.

A river squiggles inside the tighter squiggles
of contour lines. Arrows and penpoints
quicken farmstead and depot, commander
and camp, chimney stump. I perch a moment
at 4 AM where the squashed buttery
moon glints off his buttons or his horse
clicks a rock at Cupp's Ford, and it is time

for my Confederate great-grandfather
to get gut shot. And waste away, linger
three years—*the wound still suppurating*—
then leave his widow with child
who has one child. Therefore, writhing reckoner,
I ride this map like a flying carpet
and start the world for them to end again.

14. Gibson

Though you try to puppet me,
what happened to me is not

for you to know. You know it was
a Sunday night I fled. You

know (or so says the U.S.
Naval Observatory's

website) the moon, a waning
crescent, rose after midnight

and civil twilight ended
at 8:06. You can lie

on the floor and try macro-
imagining me from drained swamps,

Capitol dome, stacked stones, orchards
(my far-stretched hand even moves

your first spoonful of peaches)
and micro-imagining

the stench of fear, summer woods,
hunger, slapping vines, hard moons

on my shoeless feet, the bite
of roots as I steal away

on the long wire of longing
which hooks itself one end to

your gut, hooks the other end
to lover, brother, father,

open ocean. Longing you
know. Seven generations,

you know of, engendering
generations. Do the math.

15. Eighteenth-Century Boisseau Farmhouse
after a WPA photo

Leafless tree shadow scribbles the walls
and shadows of deflated bushes flood
the yard, an arrogant silver squalor
so pitted and clumped it seems a crowd
had barged about, then despaired of raising
a response from such a blank and pointless house.

Bare weatherboard of equivocal
color, snaggle-toothed shutters.
The place couldn't look better
for how bad it looks. Mythic,
Faulknerian. With a satisfying smack
of the cartoon. A place you'd discover

a goat enjoying the taste of mantel.
Shirts tugged from an offstage clothesline
and flung beside the swayback steps
turn out to be chickens, a couple
strutting roosters, and a lone peahen.
Someone has been working here,

patching the roof? carrying it off?
A long glaring ladder meets, tweezers-like,
its crisp leaning shadow—the two long legs
of a huge being who's about to stride
over the fields and trees, over the excellent
fires made when old wood starts to burn.

Fitz Patrick Boisseau

Odd name. Yoked way back. It was the name of my good brother Pat, the name of my talented fuckup of a father, and of his father, born thirty-eight days after his own father, John Fitz Patrick Boisseau, died of wounds received fighting for the Confederacy.

How quickly we cross the border into slavery, stepping over it as over the low wall around a grave plot or show garden. Soil gone acid from two centuries of ruinous tobacco farming, old Virginia's cash crop became its slave nursery. The standard image of the deep South—ancient mansions, trees dribbling Spanish moss—doesn't suggest how new many of those plantations were when the Civil War broke out. As vividly as my generation recollects the riots and assassinations of the 1960s, the generation of Southern whites who sent their children to war in 1861 would have remembered their own journeys from the original slave states to new states like Alabama, Mississippi, Missouri, Texas. Walking alongside the loaded wagons were slaves, many of them children, plucked from their families.

The Boisseaus and the families they married into in the South were mostly minor planters and slaveholders. My Confederate great-grandfather was a son of Peter (Virginia legislator, lawmaker when the Fugitive Slave Act passed), a son of Daniel (a teenager when the Revolution broke out). Each man sported the name "Fitzpatrick Boisseau" like a family cowlick or cancer, and over the next border we go to British citizens, to Daniel's mother, Anner Fitzpatrick, who married the grandson of the first Boisseau in the Virginia colony. Our genes are tangles of tangles.

We know only that Anner married twice, had at least ten children, lived and died in Virginia, wore dresses, drank from a cup, looked at the sky for rain. Literate or not, determined or lazy, open-hearted or emotional chit-counter, troubled or smugly shrugging at the system? I know only that she and the whole pack of them down to Jean Boisseau, who'd fled persecution in Montauban, France, in 1685, and his wife Sarah Holmes, whose family had been here already for a couple generations sucking the riches out of the soil (and lived here at that crucial moment when the labor system moved from common indentured servitude to race-based matrilineal slavery the likes of which hadn't been seen before), I know only that they lived as comfortably as they could while holding the wolf they dare not look in the eye, the solemn green eyes of their undoing. The artist Kara Walker says, "as soon as you start telling the story of racism, you start reliving the story. You keep creating a monster that swallows you." When we hear the growls of what has fed us and our children, our minds get busy trying to drown out the sound: *Couldn't help it. Not my fault. That's just the way it was back then. It's god-awful but what's to be done? The commute's brutal, but the schools. . . .* Our brains seem wired to soothe our sins.

My dead brother, Pat, spent twenty years on the warm side of brilliant, funny, kind, admirable, then thirty-three years wandering the woods of the madlands where devils hang like possums from branches, where Jesus is a volcano, and like a hank of hair your soul is yanked from your body by a passing pickup while you talk on a pay phone to your sister. In my sickest, most knotted, stinking, Gothic, grief-stricken daydreams (which I sorrily confess are not that rare), I think this name is freighted, a curse out of Hawthorne, a chancre, a festering, a ganglion grown inside the fault lines of self-justification, a seventeenth-century snarl that twists in the switchwork of our genes and erupted as my brother's suffering. His was an indescribable, casually unjust, ruthless panorama of pain that answered nothing but echoes.

Rev. James Boisseau   +   Sarah Holmes
(c. 1685 emigrates from France)
⇊

Rev. Jos. Holt + *?*
⇊

Capt. James Boisseau   +   Mary Rebecca Holt
(c. 1700–c. 1770)   (died c. 1772)
⇊

Peter Fitzpatrick + *?*
⇊

James Boisseau   +   Anner **Fitzpatrick**   +   James Yeargin
(died c. 1780)   (died 1797)
⇊

Edward Hill + *Elizabeth*
⇊

Daniel Fitzpatrick Boisseau   +   Priscilla Hill
(1760–1824)   (died 1856)
⇊

John Royall Bradley + *Mary Archer*
⇊

Peter Fitzpatrick Boisseau   +   Eliza Bradley
(c. 1800–c. 1869)   (died c. 1880)
⇊

Stith Parham + *?*
⇊

John Fitz Patrick Boisseau   +   Fannie Parham
(1829–1867)   (1833–1906)
⇊

Hugh Ryan + *Mary Gross*
⇊

Fitz Patrick Boisseau   +   Florence Ryan
(1868–1941)   (1895–1977)
⇊

Fitz Patrick Boisseau   +
(1926–1996)
⇊

Fitz Patrick (Pat) Boisseau
(1952–2005)

Thomas Tidball   +   Elizabeth Brownhill
(both arrive Philadelphia by 1715)

⇊

William Tidball   +   Mary Sheeley
(1736-1814)   ⇊   (died 1776)

David Tidball   +   Isabella McGowan
(1770-1842)   ⇊   (born 1769)

James Tidball   +   Elizabeth Cunningham
(1798-1865)   ⇊   (died 1877)

Valentine Tidball   +   Isabella Westlake
(1827-1921)   ⇊   (1834-1904)

Chas. Tidball   +   Emma Leonard
(1856-1932)   (1816-1919)

⇊

Carl Tidball   +   Irene Laurson
(1888-1937)   ⇊   (1895-1974)

June Tidball
(born 1925)

Michelle   (seven other children)

II.

A Genius for Silence

The trees insist on breaking into leaf,
blurring winter's tired distinctions.
Let's call her Eva or Madonna, and say
she died when your grandmother was two.
She'd sent no letters and no letters came.
No scared cousin showed up in overalls
in broad daylight. Sun hammering at their backs,
tongues of cotton spat from the biting husks
she studied to forget. She never told
even your great-grandfather whose thick accent
and light touch with a fiddle warmed the stories
aged aunts and uncles told in your childhood.
The spot a sapling surrenders soon heals.
In its new place the sapling proves itself
until it's synonymous with the house
it drops its leaves around. She never talked
about the slick creek bank or what she did
for the train fare. She squeezed into the corner
and met no one's eyes through all the straw-hot
morning rocking into night. Even after
rattling across the celebrated river
and the others broke out singing and passed
around sacks of cornbread, she let their gaze
inspect only her hat brim. Waving off
their kind importunities, she stayed behind

as the train emptied and echoed. She had
a passable dress, high color, good hair,
and by the time she stepped off that train—
gauging no one noticed the car she left—
she'd grown into an artist with a genius
for verisimilitude, to sketch not
the tree but the white space the tree moves through,
your lucky life the canvas she left you.

Stones Grown into His Footsoles

on the autobiography of John P. Parker, 1827–1900,
Underground Railroad conductor in Ripley, Ohio

From Richmond, Virginia,
to an Alabama frantic to fell
forests for cotton fields, the slaves stumble
and scramble as the chain yanks them
and scrapes open their scabs.
"The wilderness was all about us,
green and living." He hates it.
Hates the chestnut "in full-tasseled bloom"
where a cardinal, a "blotch of blood,"

pumps from its small body its clarion song.
Sold by his white father, sold again,
escapes, is caught, sold, escapes, sold,
learns iron mongering, buys himself,
starts a foundry along the Ohio
where he pounds metal and stares into Kentucky
where he rows at night to snatch others
from the farms they feed, a free
and freeing man who sends his children

to Oberlin and Mt. Holyoke,
in time he'll learn to steer his rage,
but now every second of his eight years
hates the pretty bird, hates the others

who mock his teeny fury as he flings rocks
and misses, grabs a stick and thrashes
azalea and rhododendron
whose pink dream of freedom bubbles
around him like bloody spit.

Found Poem

April 17, 1844, The Palladium of Liberty, *oldest known African American newspaper in Ohio*

LOST BROTHER

Major Johnston, my brother, a lad of five years of age was taken, with other slaves, to the State of Tennessee, by John Johnston, of Bartee county, North Carolina, in the year 1809, where he was left in the possession of Mr. Harry Pew, of said State. Johnston returned to North Carolina and shortly afterwards died. Mr. Pew sold my brother, Major, to a Mr. Washington Norfelt, by whom he was bound to learn the Tanner's trade. Soon after he came to the State of Ohio. Sylvia Johnston, was the name of our mother, who was married to Joseph Griffin after the death of said John Johnston, our father, by whom she had one son, named Nurval. Abba Jonnston was the name of our grand mother.

The object of this advertisement is to obtain information of said Major, where he resides, if living. Should any person acquainted with him, chance to see this description and would inform me by letter, or otherwise, would confer a lasting obligation on

JOHN JOHNSTON,
—Of Columbus, Ohio.

Outskirts of Lynchburg

In oak rings I keep
many secrets. Why talk
about them when
they're expressed

in the jerked, frayed
stem, in fruit not
of my own making.

Why talk when they've grown
part of my own heaviness.

Torches crisped my leaves.
Sooty laughter smudged the moon.

The iron taste of what
they did is laid down
in twisted bark, bit by bit,
enfolding the stem.

Monstrance

I don't believe in ghosts though I've seen
milk-steam wandering a darkened room.

I don't believe a big mind regards
all sparrows though I admire the faithful,

how crossing a street or a continent
of trouble they seem confident and frank

as stars. Cranky and cratered, I maneuver
like a moon of bright remarks.

In famous churches when the chanting
carries me into the showy moment—

hoc est enim corpus meum—the golden
rays lifted, bells shaken, incense tempest,

and I'm moved by what I don't believe,
I don't envy believers any more

than I envy beauty its ease, the ocean
its industry. The sun its long and lonely life.

The Sad Book of Fun
for Christie

At sunset you hear a few coughs
like aircraft killing their engines

and overhead thousands of sloe
bombers, the crows, are cruising in.

Some disturbance in the suburbs
or the farther farms sends them here

on schedule to drop caws and tar
the bald trees with their cheer campaign.

And we have to face whatever
it is they say, we understand.

The Good

They're beguiling as Asian dragonflies,
the leaping springbok with its lyre horns,
or the cello virtuoso who coaxes from one elbow
and four tight strings such an ocean
of low notes we feel a sudden happy need
for tears. And they're easy to spot—
for the good carry themselves with easy

radiance. They are spontaneous
and simple as springs, bright water
that souses sullen rocks. They wear
a puzzling air of calm confidence—not cocky
or brazen but assured like a tree the sun
confides with all summer long or a child
who has always worn the soft vestments

and eaten the golden bread of love.
But how they unnerve us whose boldness
is a bristling, through whom like a coal seam
a vein of badness runs, a snake that zips
across meadows and publicly
gags down the twitching mouse.
And the sun burns through a nuisance of clouds.

Sandcastle Guarded by a Cicada Shell

The rowboat is slapped by the harried lake.
The oars bob and beckon out of reach
as the storm pulls the drapes. Today
the future isn't what it used to be.

The emptied house a bell, the screen door
the clapper. Crossing the porch takes a week,
the yard a year. Only a second before . . .
The future isn't what it used to be.

A Cool Whip tub and two toy shovels
rebuke the voices that startle the geese.
Beneath the water the future aches to show
it isn't what it used to be.

Not to Mention All This Ferrous Fructiferousness

Heavy and fluffy as a pillow
of spun iron, night drifts somehow
toward the reproachful bay clattering
with daylight. Yep. Nothing's the matter.
Pull on clothes, smooth an eyebrow,

and hoist a smile. She has eight hours
then back to her familiar sour
bed and shhh to the coffee cup,
the key ring heavy to pick up.
Adjust the mirror, start the car,

back out. Four hundred and eighty
minutes to go. A cumulus cloud weighs
as much as a freight car. What glides
along buoyant and brave is ripe
with anvils crammed with space.

Time Done Is Dark

—Archibald MacLeish, Conquistador

    Childhood is a nicked black trunk
you move when you move, from attics
to basements, storage shed, crawl space,
walk-in closet. When they were in

their sixties and their mother in
her eighties, they said to her, We
are miserable, our childhoods
were miserable. And their mother?

Oldest of seventeen, four years
of school, Nothing Soup—raw milk, salt,
pepper, flour—spring snow sparking
through the wallboards, her first child

at fifteen. Childhood is a nicked
trunk you don't have to look inside
to remember. Blasted lining,
the smell of nickels. Childhood, let

it be long ago, like glaciers.

Larger than Life

The only joy is to begin.
　　　　　　—CESAR PAVESE

And so it came to pass that the immortal,
the famous, the household names visited, falling
like rain that wakes you up, and you sink
back to sleep, satisfied with the deeper course
of the dream. Through library windows
they sifted. Moonlight's cool nothing fingered

the spines, their gold names stamped beside the gold
names of rivals. Coward, lout, optimist, idler,
every virtue and flaw absolved in ink
and perfect binding. In galleries they found
their paintings in strange frames, near stranger brethren.
Sunlight splashing a cool satin skirt,

delightful wracking of a month, how paint
could carry the right sense of encroachment
and slippage—seemed unavailing, accusing
like the empty plate of an absent guest.
Beneath a glowing red EXIT a sleeping guard
coughed, stretched, and revealed in his hand

the yellow leather of a banana peel.
In the streets more treasure, cupcake wrapper
somersaulting, roofs pitching the wind
down their backs, trees tasting the rush of rain.
Just to touch the unaccountable flippant weeds . . .
But bargaining cannot return a body.

Night Valley

for Tracy and Marjorie

Rosemary and wild fennel *krst, krst*
underfoot. When we stop, the fragrance
settles and waits. Far below, a crawl

of car lights scrolls between Florence
and Pistoia, following a road so old
the olive trees we look through

appear interlopers. The gentling
of an ancient place seasons our play
with *zanzare*, rolling the word

for mosquitoes around in our mouths
like a gulp of wine to praise
how they add that necessary pinch

of mockery which keeps beauty
from stupidity and reminds us
nothing alone is perfect. A glance

seizes a distance it would take
a day to travel—inscrutable
Etruscans, grave centurions,

Huns and Lombards, St. Francis
on a donkey, Medici popes
trailing brocaded buglers, pockets

of partisans, U.S. army tanks, tour
buses with red curtains drawn. Ripe
fruit bursts. We are born for longing.

Bird Shadow on Window Glass
    F.P.B. (1952–2005)

In the recital hall the last note
        of the soprano flickers like dew.
The dry canyon expresses the quick
        vanished river. The tongue squinches
at the memory, tearing

        into the ginny lime. And the way
the sidewalk burns hours after
        the sun's gone down, my hand
is strobing from stroking his hair,
        his hand still capable of grasping.

Recriminating Rags of Sunlight

And don't forget to stay together.

At that time there lived a brother
and sister who followed a trail of flints
into the woods. They were curious,
but it wasn't fatal. The trees stood

shoulder to shoulder drippling their hushed
needles. Bark crumble, gills of mushrooms,
and there was room for speculation.
A whistle, a flap, something wouldn't

show itself, then a small clearing did—
snapped trees and blue asters fringed a good
granite boulder huge as God that he
climbed to look farther in. Don't forget.

Warm stone, but when she turned to go on,
he had stepped through. For a long while she
stood thinking he was sure to come back.

Hard Weather

Who would have thought my shriveled heart
Could have recovered greenness?

—GEORGE HERBERT, "THE FLOWER"

Wrung and wintered, she pulled in
among the bikes then stopped to watch
the exhaust unraveling in the rearview
the way someone watches a freighter

diminish and go. How little a thing
to poke the garage opener, erase
the bright foggy windows, rattle
of dishes, husband, daughter setting the table.

They say it's a gentle falling,

leaves picked off a tree one by one
until it stands clean and ready.
A warm sleepiness soaks you.
We love best the dark we make ourselves.

Pertinacious Seedheads

Stuck on the side of the road,
you start to feel the occasional
passing car or truck that bucks
your car in its gravel spot

is the mistaken one. The surface
of your imperial attention
is breeched by barbwire and grasses.
The fields assert themselves.

Someone lives here. A coffee cup
on the porch rail. Staked tomatoes.
How quickly you lose consequence
beside the hoed and ratified rows.

Inkling

When I'm doodling an ink pathway
in my usual style, I'm bound
to end with intermarried squares,
a mazy Renaissance garden

where a hostage princess can pine
contentedly. A moving pen
is memory's wormhole. This morning
inking up a page's corner,

I land in a remote moment
where rafts of numbers have been wrecked
on the slate sea. An armada
of arithmetic was sent out

against me. And at the big desk
on the horizon, the rising
thunderhead of Sister Roberts—
she's wiry as her steel glasses,

but her face is blank and blanker
the faces of forty others
I weathered eight years with. Details
have been sifted down to a red

shirt up-aisle, scarred toe of a shoe
of the kid who sits beside me.
With these sufficient snatches, I
resurrect what matters to me,

the time travel of suddenly
knowing what being ten feels like,
coercion, obedience, small
acts of defiance to withstand

another afternoon. Beyond
the bank of windows are my strong
parents and my living brother,
offered as ransom for my release.

After a While, Time Passed

Leaving the icy blank, Tempus Incognito,
unimagined by Caesar or Pope Gregory,
like a scout in the ordinary black boots
of ordinals, today's date crosses the border
of the morning paper and sets up camp

for vanguard and arsenal. A calendar
makes neat fiction. Each day its separate cage
like doggies stacked at a dog show. The cage
can't stretch for *this day will never end,* can't
collapse like snow that loses its will to pose

on the wet branch. How long's it been, inside
this dim and dripping cabin? It's hard telling
time hiding inside an avalanche, hard
to hear the stranger coming though the rain
of nails. He blinks the ice out of his eyes.

I don't know him but recognize his face
as I read the days since my brother died.

A Porchful of Presbyterians
the Tidballs, 1903

Seeping limestone, springhead,
hanging valleys, and glaciers
shed from granite faces, branches
branch back and are lost

maiden names of great-
grandmothers. A river says
of its ancestry what we all say.
I came from somewhere.

Runnel of cowlick, small feet,
intimidated smile
(my mean streak I've traced
in other lines). The rain trickled

off stricken pines. Whelks
of streambed were smoothed away.
The sun passed the time
roof to roof and was drunk up

by wet plate, the dark diamonds
in that lattice, these long dark
socks my mother's father,
a boy in knickers, doesn't seem

to mind though it's August.
His parents he sits between
on the wide steps, his grandparents,
the old abolitionists (Our Golden

Wedding) in large carved chairs,
uncles, aunts, cousins have opened
a channel of their attention
for the implicit photographer,

an eclipse under hot cloth,
his hand raised to say steady,
steady now. On the river
the ship is launched with the tide

tugged by the moon that keeps
time adamant and airless—
only a little while longer to put
our hand to the cave damp.

Flying with the Eyes of a Satellite
    for TSS

How quickly looking
is not enough, how

soon beauty quickens
the longing to slip

my fingers inside
a satiny pleat

of cloud, slide my tongue
on the vertebrae

of mountains where lakes
dimple the valleys

and take the firred slopes
in their hushed mirrors.

Here a delta tastes
the first reach of salt,

an obliging bay
accepts the gentle

onslaught of the sea's
bare breast and a thrust

of sandbar softens
faraway. Above

Earth a hundred miles
we know what gods know

of love. Remotely.
With only the eyes,

such cool and thorough
knowing satisfies

theorists, perhaps,
or the terribly

good, but we're a mess
of plasma and flash

ruby electric
storms as we bloom new

galaxies and taste
the body's knowledge.

& if & if

Tiny word, front vowel and fricative,
it lifted willowy in my brother's
hospital room wormy with cords
and monitors, feeds and drips,
the doctors on call and the residents,

interns, students, nurses (adept Jennifer,
lovely Rolando), respiratory therapists
(gentle Victor). *If,* a word sturdily
delicate, feather barb, hook of hope.

Ode to the Tongue

Wet bucking bed. Flippant
surfboard that makes its own waves.

Conveyor of claptrap, hot air, moonshine,
and truth: warm sweet smooth.
It guides our first taste of the good—
spontaneous milk—and flumes
through us our mother tongue.

Wag it, lose it, hold it, bite it, slip it.
Stick it firmly in the cheek. Hanging out.
Tied and twisted. The cat got it.
Gimme a lick. Chew it over.
Come on, what's wrong? Spit it out!

Sun, stars, eternal horizon—
distance has its share of champions.

I praise this wiggler rooted to our heads
who teaches taste is touch. Open up
and take in the other. Oyster sluice. Gritty
grammars. The slurp of linguine.
Chalky pill. Taste your own medicine, pal!

And when we praise precision,
let's be frank as the hawk that buries
its face in the surgical strike.

Die Zwei Ist Zweifel
("Two Is Doubt")

—Friedrich Rückert

There is one God and one God only.
He fills up everywhere, bread dough
brimming the blue bowl, so there's no
room for him to feel lonely.

There are two kinds of people in the world.

Of the one thousand things to see before
you die, like the Grand Canyon and Big Ben,
you won't find among them this squirrel,
a ball of gray yarn bouncing across the yard,
but look how quickly your brain absorbs it,
a penny fluttering to the lake bottom.

You can count on the fingers
of one hand.
We were born digital.

On the 1002nd night Sheherezad
wrote a poem. Climbing the foothills
of his ribcage, her tongue followed the rhyme

she lay down. Clatter of peacock quills,
strange familiar cry . . .

It's handy
how there are ten commandments.

There are those who break things
into parts. Let's stand together at the window
as the rain topples the tulips and drop
by drop eases up and over
the birdbath, makes marks, leaves none.

III.

Across the Borderlands, the Wind

> *My present field of consciousness is a centre surrounded by a*
> *fringe that shades insensibly into a subconscious of more.*
>
> —WILLIAM JAMES

Fringe planet. Shifty river. Bright shade.

The notes between the notes we hear
loud as the bird song. Bright shade
then morning blaze. This time of day
our shadows grow us tall and even
the seams between close-laid stones
in the dawn street are touched,
light-honed and articulated.

Mountain range and threadbare frontier.
Foray, skirmish, raid. By war, treaty,
algebra and surveyors in knee britches.
Stay out of my yard! City limits, state line,
double electric fence, high wall,
and watchtower where bored soldiers
insult each other's sisters on schedule.

* * *

The eastern woods give way to the long grass
that gives way to the short-grass prairie,

gumbo lily, whistle of the meadow lark
riding and falling on the wind.

Last gas for ninety-three miles.

* * *

I'm half asleep as I watch them crossing
the border into Kansas. Coming out
of the night woods, they're the dark
coming apart, the avant dark, ahead
of a dawn ordinary to an old man
who presses a cheek against his cow's flank.
Warm milk threads his fingers, a breeze
drags the dust around the farmyard

where Quantrill's raiders ride in.
In earshot of the town they'll burn, they don't
shoot him like the nine others but club him
with the butt-end of a Sharp's carbine.
A flash of wood, the sleek shaft gripped,
and I look away, again the aerial view,
the stream of riders like wind through grass

as they gallop up the streets of Lawrence.
The tent tops of the recruit encampment
(a plot now shaded by a parking structure),
I hover till they're the size of screw heads,
and the pursuit and slaughter and fire
jumping roof to roof become a gray

business of graphite and margins
gradated by the thickets of sleep.

* * *

The tideline makes the gull bold
to snatch a sandwich from a child's hand,
and the sandpiper anxious,
drilling its shining self on the wet berm.

Wetlands, momentary land
of leggy tadpoles.

* * *

When they was kids, him and his sister
would beg their daddy to drive down

State Line Road, and they'd stretch out
in the back seat of the Hudson,

heads in Kansas, feet in Missouri
where the peachy moon was rising.

* * *

Ordinance and algebra. Along the dammed
and channeled river where I grew up
you could look down from Eden Park
on Kentucky. The bare rooftops

and vertiginous spires of the poor
former slave state offended
the good sense we had to be born
in Ohio. And yet the crooked smile,

like someone who'd brushed up
against a splendid outlaw,
Dad would make a wistful crack
about his grandfather's rumored
riches, slaves lost in old Virginia.

* * *

Latching on to a likely host
wafting past, it sucks a door
out of the cell wall: not alive but living
off life, the virus attacks passively

like in-laws. Next thing you know
you're tripping over their suitcases
and they've broken up your bed
for fires under their roaring kettles.

* * *

A note pinned to a dead jayhawker,
"You come to hunt bushwackers.
Now you ar skelpt." When the worst

border war guerilla was killed,
Bloody Bill Anderson, they reported
eleven human scalps fluttered like ribbons

from his bridle band. Tucked in his watch case
a lock from his buxom wife. Townsfolk
lined up to have a picture with the corpse.

* * *

Oxbow lake.
When the river

shifted, it left
an elbow of water

and this here
part of the state

was stranded
and stubbornized.

* * *

The way smoke rising from many fires
is blown in tangles and scuds
like a blanket dragged across a floor
of rooftops and competing spires, the chiming

from churches on one side of the Green Line
wed the singing from minarets
on the other as the crackle of vespas
and blaring Euro hiphop tried to amp up

the coolness factor of the strobing stores
of the South Nicosia shopping district
that gave way to the silence of warehouses,
workshops where a few machines whined

under low lights. When I walked past,
Western woman with a water bottle,
workers glanced up then back to the making
of laminated furniture for seashore condos,

then a dead end at the Green Line, barrel
barricades, streets of weeds, walls crumbling
like cake and feral cats wending through
the way looping thoughts wake a sleeper.

Trees eagered from de-glazed windows.
I heard a cough. At my elbow, wedged
into a slit of shade, a young man with a gun
and a water bottle—a sweating sunburned blond

in a UN uniform—we'd startled each other,
and now humbled by the heat, befuddled
by a goofy sense of guilt, we scrambled
to nod obliquely and look away.

　　　* * *

At the last station before Holland,
a voice on the speakers announced,
"Alle Juden heraus." The train hissed,
doors slammed, and because Bertha,
the oldest, had the presence of mind

to warn her sisters to sit still, they made
Amsterdam, and later the Twin Cities
where they lived to old age. Their neighbors—
who'd obeyed, gathered up their coats
and stepped off—were not heard from again.

* * *

Drips and drains. Late night, deep
into that frayed frontier, the ICU's
screens measuring his body's forecast

in slim crests and dips: Still, still, still,
there's comfort even in the steady
mechanical breathing, the stalwart

ventilator leashed to my brother,
the terrible comfort I will take
from time slipping at the door.

* * *

Ticking off centuries like seconds,
the great slow plates clutch

and shift intent as lovers, seas open,
mountains climb and fold. Elephants

broke fences, monkeys raced
for high ground: everybody except people

knew it was coming. For weeks after
the quake, the earth rang like a bell.

     *   *   *

From a dock on a lake
on an island in a lake
I dive into the stars,
scatter them and gather them
between my arms and legs,
then watch them heal themselves
in place. Venus rebounds
on the water, the wet dock,
the low islands of my breasts:
we're all in a reflective mood.

Even centuries past the fringe
planets like Pluto, the sun,
dim as the last
gas station we left miles back,
tugs and grips,
oh, the gravitas of edges.

     *   *   *

When he blew clean
the borderline between stone

and body grown from stone
Michelangelo's eyelashes

were dusted with desire
like the hair of a honey bee.

* * *

The tiny wellsprings dimpling
the ridges of our fingertips mist

the air that touches us. Lying in bed,
tracing a vein that crosses your arm,

I'm the ocean in love with the sky.
Seamless ripples, a rise and response,

clouds are the trade of touch, exchange
rate of kisses. Never, *There*, or *Once*

and for all though we sweat and murmur,
That should keep you fucked a while.

South Dakota Field Trip
in the Titanothere beds of the White River Badlands

Nowhere in the world
could you find a word.
Constellations swam overhead nameless
and ungodded. No one complained
about the weather's same old, same old,
recorded, just the same, in strongholds
of ice and stonestacks that wrote the epics
of the epochs. India hankered after Asia
in quivers and the Himalayas
were born and born. Hawaii's nipples
steamed in the ocean. Florida lay rippling
beneath shallow seas, dreaming
of fountains and skies that streamed
cranes, kites and pink flamingos.
And here savannahs rose

and spread their ample grasses
for the mouths of the earliest grazers
we dig for among a thousand gray knuckles—
the Badlands. Not a bird, not a whining truck
nudges the quiet. Even the wind is soundless,
leaning against me its huge roundness
as I stroke a clump of shale, coax

it from its dusty stone clothes
until it reveals itself as bone.

Here are the chalky caves
where the blood wheeled. This smooth plain
the cortex, its enamel riven like porcelain.
The skull is longer than my arm, longer,
but as we brush and try to draw
it out, the skull crumbles and slides
back into silence.

Bigger than a bread truck,
ugly as a truck wreck,
these big mothers
nursed their humongous young
here for millions of years
(though here wasn't yet here),
each spring silkened with the smell of milk,
and were gone for millions
before we climbed from trees, children
gripping our backs, and tried
the page laid open to unfamiliar skies.

When I Consider

Big eye and little eye. Ego, ego.

Consolation. A form of feeling. Sun-
light ramps through the window. Hello, hello!
I'm coming and coming every second,
ninety-three million miles with my letters.

It's soothing to hold this weighty ancient,
a chunk of fossilized skull rewritten
with hairline rivers. The smooth enamel
my thumb inspects urges me to touch next
the spongy places where the marrow glowed
like shelves of jelly jars the sun put up.

Satisfying. The fossil does enough.
When I put it down, my hands come away
talcumed with time.

                    Considering is star-
gazing. Looking far in, back, or beyond,
and I begin the drifting fall, milkweed
whose microgram seed rudders it, as I
let the chalk pillars of my grief collapse.

My brother, father, friends, even my own
brevity.

Let go, we're taught, just lean back,
spread your arms. Give yourself to the water
and the water will hold you.

NOTES

Epigraph, from Cleophas C. O'Harra's *The White River Badlands*, 1920,
   John Strong Newberry was the first geologist to map the Grand
   Canyon, 1858.

I.

"A Sunday in God-Years," the Presbyterian minister John Rankin told
   Harriet Beecher Stowe the story of the woman who'd run away
   from a Kentucky farm. Around her, Stowe created Eliza for *Uncle
   Tom's Cabin*. The woman, whose child was going to be sold, fled
   from a Kentucky farm, across the soft ice of the Ohio, chased by
   dogs, and made it to Canada; she along with hundreds (even
   thousands) of others was helped by the Rankin family of Ripley,
   Ohio, who kept a light burning in their house that stood high
   over the Ohio River, visible for miles. John and Jean Rankin, orig-
   inally from the South, came to Ohio in the 1820s after breaking
   with Southern Presbyterians over slavery, and began to lay the
   rails for the Underground Railroad through Ohio. The term
   "Underground Railroad" is believed to have originated in Ripley.
   With its feet touching the South and its head Canada, Ohio was
   probably the most important route for escaped slaves, especially
   after the Fugitive Slave Act (1850).

   Rankin's *Letters on Slavery* published in the 1820s in Ripley
   inspired the radical abolitionist William Lloyd Garrison, who
   reprinted them in his newspaper the *Liberator* in 1832, the same
   year that Harriet Beecher Stowe came to Ohio with her family.
   Her father, Lyman Beecher, had been named president of Lane
   Theological Seminary in Cincinnati, downriver from Ripley; he
   brought with him Emily Dickinson's grandfather, grandmother,
   and young aunts. Samuel Dickinson left Lane within a few years
   evidently due to incompetence and went north to Western
   Reserve College where he died in 1838. In 1834 students at Lane,
   many of whom came from the South, tried to put their antislav-
   ery views into action and started night classes for the free blacks

of Cincinnati. The close contacts between whites and blacks out-
raged many white Cincinnatians, and they threatened to burn
down the seminary. The panicked trustees imposed strict rules
on the students, abolishing their antislavery society; when the
trustees refused to discuss the new rules with the Lane Rebels,
fifty-one students walked out; dozens went to the newly estab-
lished Oberlin College, which admitted students of color.

I'm indebted to many researchers, especially Stuart Sprague,
ed., *His Promised Land: The Autobiography of John P. Parker, Former Slave
and Conductor on the Underground Railroad* (cf. n. "Stones Grown into
his Footsoles"), as well as Anne Hagedorn, *Beyond the River: The
Untold Story of the Heroes of the Underground Railroad;* Wilbur H.
Siebert, "Ohio's Underground Trails," map; Nikki M. Taylor,
Frontier's of Freedom: Cincinnati's Black Community 1802–1868.

"A Reckoning"

"The Debt," until black slavery made it possible for Europeans
to plant sugar cane in their new colonies, sugar, a luxury for
only the uber-rich, was controlled as a medicine. The aro-
mas floating from sugar refineries in the Near East lead the
Crusaders to the Holy Land. "[I]t was said the magnificent
royal palaces of Madrid and Toledo, built by Emperor
Charles V, were paid for entirely by the profits of sugar"
(Maguelonne Toussaint-Samat, *The History of Food*). When
characters in nineteenth-century novels visit their concerns
in the West Indies, they're inspecting their sugar plantations.

"Ruminator," La Rochelle, etc., ports in the international slave
market.

"No Trespassing," off Genito Road, Amelia County, Virginia;
enter 37 27'N, 77 52W on Google Earth and you will hover
over the 1500 acres they owned. My rental car had New
Hampshire plates, and the neighbors thereabouts seemed
unfriendly behind their curtains.

"Meanwhile," 1834: see also note above for "A Sunday in God-
Years." To be fair to my mother's paternal line, the Tidballs
(Presbyterians, who arrived before 1715) opposed slavery and
served in the Union army. Other lines (Larsons, Laursons,

Ryans, Grosses, Leonards, Kochs, Francks) had not yet come to American and reaped the benefits of whiteness.

"Reward," Half-way House, the major stop between Richmond and Petersburg, still serves lunch and dinner.

"The Subscriber," there are many ways to be wrong and as many to be gutless. I know next to nothing about my great-great-grandfather Peter except his resume: went to William and Mary, had six sons and one daughter, bought and sold real estate and human property. He and Eliza, his wife, sold their farm along the Appomattox during the Civil War. And with it the fifty-six men, women, and children they lived beside? He was a respected man, signed his name in court so nieces could marry and wills be probated. He served a couple terms as delegate to the Virginia General Assembly. His sister, Harriet, was married to John Winston Jones, a Jacksonian Democrat and speaker to the U.S. House when fellow Democrat President James K. Polk pushed for the territorial expansion Thoreau so reviled and which eventually lead to the Civil War.

But what did he feel about his life? Peter, who gave me a sixteenth of my genes, remains a smudge and cipher, but the closely observed paragraph he wrote makes Gibson vivid. Not only do I have a sense of what Gibson looked like but also who he was: sensibly cautious ("very polite when spoken to"), determined ("carried off all his clothing"), loving and lonely (he was going to find his father), enterprising and talented (he'd worked in town). He was not a man to be knocked off his unshakeable sense of self— so says the hat with the crape.

"Catalogue," the number 56 for slaves held comes from a transcription by Tom Blake, July 2003, of the 1860 slave census.

"Two Wills in Old Virginia," cf. "Both thy bondmen and thy bondmaids, which thou shalt have, shall be of the heathen that are round about you; of them shall ye buy bondmen and bondmaids.

"Moreover of the children of the strangers that do

sojourn among you, of them shall ye buy, and of their families that are with you, which they begat in your land: and they shall be your possession.

"And ye shall take them as an inheritance for your children after you, to inherit them for a possession they shall be your bondmen for ever" (Leviticus, 25: 44–47).

"Before the Age of Aerial Bombardment," Bvt. Lt. Col. G. L. Gillespie, "Battle-fields of Fisher's Hill and Cedar Creek," map (1873). The Battle of Cedar Creek was part of Sheridan's fall 1864 Shenandoah Valley campaign, following Grant's orders to turn the valley into a "barren waste . . . so that crows flying over it for the balance of this season will have to carry their provender with them." When you stand on the porch of the visitors' center (bullets dug from the battlefield are in a basket by the cash register for a buck each), you're in earshot of the traffic on I-81 turning to I-66 into D.C. and can still see notches cut into the hills where lookouts before the battle cut down trees to be able to signal each other.

"Fitz Patrick Boisseau," about the soil in Virginia, cf. Charles Dickens, *American Notes*, 1842: "The tract of country through which [the train from Fredericksburg to Richmond] takes its course was once productive; but the soil has been exhausted by the system of employing a great amount of slave labour in forcing crops, without strengthening the land: and it is now little better than a sandy desert overgrown with trees. Dreary and uninteresting as its aspect is, I was glad to the heart to find anything on which one of the curses of this horrible institution has fallen; and had greater pleasure in contemplating the withered ground, than the richest and most thriving cultivation in the same place could possibly have afforded me.

"In this district, as in all others where slavery sits brooding (I have frequently heard this admitted, even by those who are its warmest advocates): there is an air of ruin and decay abroad, which is inseparable from the system. The barns and outhouses are mouldering away; the sheds are patched and half roofless; the log cabins . . . are squalid in the last degree. There is no look of decent comfort anywhere. The miserable stations by the railway side, the great wild wood yards, whence the engine is supplied with fuel; the negro children rolling on the ground before the cabin doors, with dogs and pigs; the biped beasts of burden slinking past: gloom and dejection are upon them all."

I am deeply indebted to Andrew Boisseau's meticulous research on the Boisseaus. Andrew's great-grandfather was the youngest brother of my great-grandfather John Fitz Patrick Boisseau (cf. n. above to "The Subscriber" and "Before the Age of Aerial Bombardment"). The Boisseaus were Huguenots. After Louis XIV's Revocation of the Edict of Nantes, and the killing of his father, uncle, and brother, the young Jean (later James), his brother, and mother fled to England, where Jean signed a receipt for twenty pounds on November 11, 1689, for payment to emigrate and serve as a minister to a Virginia parish.

Having sent packing the Catholic French sympathizer James II to the court at Versailles, William and Mary in the Glorious Revolution had taken the throne in 1688, and the English Protestants were eager to spread loyal ministers in the colonies. Legend has it Jean and his brother Joseph (along with Joseph's new wife Mathlide H. S. Sausussure) left England on two separate ships, which lost each other in a storm; both thought the other dead until their grandchildren met many years later. This story seems phony although Joseph and Mathilde, it is claimed, owned a sugar plantation on St. Christopher in the West Indies, and who would own up to that if they didn't have to?

The wars of religion found an ironic twist in 1925 when my aging Virginian grandfather married a daughter of German and Irish Catholics, and the battles over slavery found a twist when their son, my father, married my mother, of an old Ohio Presbyterian Abolitionist family, and this couple raised their children Catholic.

Such fine points disintegrate in an instant—as when you cross the high, high bridge from the train station over the Tarn River into Montauban, feeling the wind nudge and knock at you, you take the route the king's troops marched to attack the Huguenot stronghold, stepping along intricate patterns of black and white rounded stones. The white are ancient granite washed down from the Pyrenees to the Garonne River; the black are newer basalt washed down the Tarn from the Auvergne, home to France's many extinct volcanoes which began erupting 20 million years ago, about the time the Himalayas started to rise.

II.

"Stones Grown into His Footsoles," "[T]he interior [of Alabama] was covered with a dense woods, which was being cleared as rapidly as possible for cotton fields. In the north the clearing of a few acres was the task of years. The white pioneers took their time and did the job comfortably. Not so Alabama. Cotton was in demand, each field was a gold mine, so that Virginia, Kentucky, and Missouri, where cotton could not be raised, were the new breeding places for slaves, who were sold south like mules to clear away their forests" (Parker, *His Promised Land*). A cruel alignment of events spread slavery: the closing of the U.S. international slave trade (1808) which spiked the internal slave trade, the spread of the cotton gin, and the land grab after the War of 1812 that drove native peoples out of the warm places where cotton could thrive.

Parker helped hundreds of slaves escape over the Ohio, often relaying them up the hill to the Rankins (see n. "A Sunday in God-Years"),whose hiding spot under their front porch could hide maybe a dozen of those in flight. Parker's account of the risks and secrecy of outmaneuvering the slave catchers who lived all around them explains why the hundred of lines of the railroad have been disappeared to history. The people who worked it didn't risk talk.

"Found Poem," the county in North Carolina was probably Bertie. I haven't found if John found his brother. John, Major, as well as John Parker, above, and Frederick Douglass, not to mention Thomas Jefferson's children, were enslaved by their own fathers. No wonder Harriet Beecher Stowe said that "nobody could begin to think and read on [slavery] without becoming piratically insane." As to the year 1809, note how this is one year after the abolition in the U.S. of the international slave trade.

The *Palladium of Liberty* was published in Ohio from 1843 to 1844 by editor David Jenkins, a free black from Virginia who came to Ohio in 1837. Jenkins was an operator in the Underground Railroad, a Union infantry recruiter, and after the war, was appointed to the Freedman's Bureau in Mississippi and elected to the Mississippi legislature in 1875 but died, of reported natural causes, at age sixty-six in 1877, the year of the infamous compromise with the Southern Democrats which put Ohio Republican Rutherford B. Hayes in the White House after a disputed election, ended Reconstruction, and rolled back civil rights for blacks.

"Monstrance," *"hoc est enim corpus meum,"* "for this is my body." The Latin phrase is thought to be the origin of "hocus pocus."

"Sandcastle Guarded by a Cicada Shell," refrain taken from a "Dear Abby" headline.

"Night Valley," thoughts on scale, from that hill on a clear day you can see Giotto's Campanile and the Duomo about four millimeters tall.

"Bird Shadow on Window Glass," the final line comes from Keats's last poem, "This Living Hand."

"After a While, Time Passed," we're still using the calendar Pope Gregory XIII ordered in 1582 which supplanted Julius Caesar's of 45 BC. England, and its colonies, didn't adopt the new calendar until 1752; for a hundred and seventy years, if you crossed the Channel from France, on March 15, for instance, you would arrive the same day in Dover on March 4.

"& if & if," thanks also to Dr. Michel, Craig, Raymond, David, Dr. Keith, Dr. Gary, Dr. Sarah, Dr. Mario, Dr. Rainey, Dr. Chris, Jim, Dr. Patel, Emily, Denise, Bill, Brandy, Michele, Wade, Sallon, Erica, and Karen.

III.

"Across the Borderlands, the Wind," the bushwhackers included, before the war ended, the young terrorist Jesse James. Edward E. Leslie, *The Devil Knows How to Ride: The True Story of William Clarke Quantrill and His Confederate Raiders:* At the first reunion of bushwhackers in

Blue Springs, Missouri, (now a Kansas City suburb) in 1898 many senators and congressmen gave speeches, but Frank James, urged to say a few words, declined, "allowing as how, while he had done many foolish things in his life, he had never done anything that dumb." The Blue Springs fall festival even into the 1990s was called the Bushwhackers Festival: rides, carnival games, parade.

That said, one must also keep in mind that the methods of Union supporters and antislavery activists, the jayhawkers, were often equally brutal; the Civil War began on the Missouri-Kansas border with atrocities like John Brown and sons' attack on six men whose families found their bodies dismembered—ears, hands, arms hacked off.

After the Missouri River bends to the east and slices Missouri in half, the state line becomes a dotted line, then a street, then a line again, heading straight for the Arkansas-Oklahoma border, which is the direction that Confederate general Sterling Price retreated with his ragged troops after being defeated in October 1864 (a week after the Battle of Cedar Creek in Virginia) in the Battle of Westport, the site of which now contains a shopping district in Kansas City, with many high-end shops. The football and basketball rivalry between the Universities of Missouri and Kansas is still often referred to as "The Border War."

The Northwest Ordinance of 1787 (which established the territory that is now Ohio, Michigan, Indiana, Illinois, and Wisconsin) banned slavery. Eden Park is located in Cincinnati. I am also indebted to Nancy Henley and Mark Jarman for some of their family stories.

"Alle Juden heraus": all Jews out.

"South Dakota Field Trip," "The skull [of the titanothere] is particularly grotesque and noteworthy. It is a long, low, saddle-shaped affair, with remarkable nasal prominences at the extreme end, bearing in most species, especially the later ones, powerful bony protuberances. The protuberances are commonly spoken of as horn or horn cores, but there is much doubt as to there ever having been sheathed in horn," O'Harra, *The White River Badlands.*